Momotaro and the Oni

Story written by Adrian Bradbury
Illustrated by Tim Archbold

Speed Sounds

Consonants *Ask children to say the sounds.*

f	l	m	n	r	s	v	z	sh	th	ng
ff	ll	mm	nn	(rr)	ss	ve	zz			nk
ph	le	mb	kn	wr	se		se			
			gn		c		s			
					ce					

b	c	d	g	h	j	p	qu	t	w	x	y	ch
(bb)	k	dd	gg		g	(pp)		tt	(wh)			tch
	ck		gu		ge							
					dge							

Each box contains one sound but sometimes more than one grapheme.
*Focus graphemes for this story are **circled**.*

Vowels

Ask children to say the sounds in and out of order.

a	e ea	i	o	u	ay a͡-e a ai aigh	ee e͡-e ea e y	igh i͡-e ie i y	ow o͡-e oa o oe

oo u͡-e ue ew	oo	ar	or oor ore aw au	air are	ir ur er	ou ow	oy oi	ire	ear	ure

Word endings

t<u>ure</u> s<u>ure</u>	<u>ous</u> e<u>ous</u> ci <u>ous</u> ti <u>ous</u>	ab<u>le</u> ab<u>ly</u> ib<u>le</u> ib<u>ly</u>	**tion**

Story Green Words

Ask children to read the words first in Fred Talk and then say the word.

trail   swung   huge   blew   cruel   wild   key*

Ask children to say the syllables and then read the whole word.

Mom|o|tar|o   de|struc|tion   O|ni   a|shamed   dump|ling

sec|tion   a|ttack   flabb|er|gas|ted   mon|key*

so|lu|tion*   ex|haus|tion*   con|fu|sion*

Ask children to read the root first and then the whole word with the suffix.

appear → appeared   creature → creatures   sudden → suddenly

reply → replied   plunge → plunging   fence → fences

taste → tasty   frighten → frightening   scamper → scampered

* Challenge Words

Vocabulary Check

Discuss the meaning (as used in the story) after the children have read each word.

	definition:	sentence:
solution	answer	He needed to find a solution to the problem.
section	part	When they reached the next section of the river...
scampered	ran	A dog scampered over.
exhaustion	tiredness	"Stop! Stop!" they sobbed in exhaustion.
flabbergasted	shocked	... the Oni were flabbergasted to see a monkey, a dog, a bird and a boy!

Red Words

Ask children to practise reading the words across the rows, down the columns and in and out of order clearly and quickly.

bought	through	where	worse
they	above	two	are
great	who	through	everyone
walk	their	by	one
mother	come	thought	were

8

Momotaro and the Oni

Momotaro lived with his parents, on a tiny farm by a river. One day three cruel Oni appeared. The Oni were huge, frightening creatures who left a trail of destruction.

On the first night, they stamped on the fences. On the second night, they kicked over the barn. On the third night, they chased the animals.

"It's time to take action!" cried Momotaro.

Over dinner, Momotaro thought hard. He needed to find a solution to the problem. Suddenly he looked up. "I'm going to fight the Oni," he said.

"But they're so big and strong!" said his parents, horrified. "You can't stop them!"

But Momotaro had made up his mind. He swept his tasty fish dumplings into his bag, said a quick farewell to his parents then marched out of the door. He was going to teach the Oni a lesson!

Momotaro followed the path along the river. After a while he became hungry and stopped to eat a dumpling.

A monkey swung down from a branch. "Where are you going?" asked the monkey.

"To fight the Oni!" replied Momotaro.

"Give me one of those dumplings and I'll come with you to help."

So Momotaro gave the monkey a dumpling and the two walked on together.

When they reached the next section of the river, they stopped again to eat.

A dog scampered over. "Where are you two going?" asked the dog.

"To fight the Oni!" replied Momotaro.

"Give me one of those dumplings and I'll come with you to help."

So Momotaro gave the dog a dumpling and the three walked on together.

Much later that day, they stopped again. A parrot flapped down from a tree. "Where are you three going?" asked the parrot.
Well, I'm sure you know what happened next...

It was dark when they reached the huge house where the Oni lived. The parrot flew in through a window and stole the door key. The monkey turned the key in the lock.

Without hesitation, Momotaro pushed open the door. Then the dog blew out the lamps, plunging the house into darkness.

The Oni, not the cleverest of creatures, were shocked. The parrot flapped its wings at their heads, the monkey pulled their ears and the dog snapped at their legs. (Not to mention Momotaro prodding at them with his stick.) In the confusion they thought they were under attack from lots of wild animals.

"Stop! Stop!" they sobbed in exhaustion. "We give in!"

When Momotaro lit the lamps, the Oni were flabbergasted to see a monkey, a dog, a bird and a boy! They felt so silly that they had been tricked.

The Oni were so ashamed that they never dared to show their faces along the river, ever again.

Questions to talk about

Ask children to TTYP each question using 'Fastest finger' (FF) or 'Have a think' (HaT).

p.9	(HaT)	Why did Momotaro think it was time to take action?
p.10	(HaT)	Why did Momotaro leave his farm?
pp.11–12	(FF)	What did the animals want in return for their help?
p.13	(HaT)	What do you think happened when Momotaro met the parrot?
p.14	(HaT)	The Oni thought they were being attacked by wild animals. Why did they think this?
p.15	(FF)	What happened when Momotaro lit the lamps?
p.15	(FF)	How did the Oni feel at the end of the story?

Questions to read and answer

(Children complete without your help.)

1. Momotaro lived **by a forest / in a town / by a river**.

2. Momotaro packed his **fish dumplings / fish pie / fish fingers** in a bag.

3. The monkey asked **"What time is it?" / "Where are you going?" / "What's your name?"**

4. **The dog / The monkey / Momotaro** blew out the lamps.

5. The parrot flapped its wings at the Oni's **legs / heads / feet**.

Speedy Green Words

show	gave	tree	night
eat	river	open	action
know	while	looked	sure
first	door	ears	path
barn	three	time	house